ELLIVATE

Unlock Your Potential for
Extraordinary Achievement
and Transform Your Success

By Crystal Ellison

Ellivate

Acknowledgements

I would like to express my deepest appreciation to an extraordinary individual who has played an indispensable role in my life and journey. This acknowledgment is dedicated to my remarkable husband, Duane. Duane, your unwavering love, support, and encouragement have been the driving force behind my accomplishments. As a loving and devoted husband, you have created a space filled with warmth and inspiration, allowing me to flourish both personally and professionally. As a father, your guidance and dedication have been instrumental in shaping our family's values and nurturing our children's growth. Your role as a pillar of strength and compassion has enriched their lives and continues to be a source of inspiration for us all. In the realm of business ownership, you have been my guiding light, always reminding me that regrets lie in missed opportunities rather than the outcome of taking risks. Your wisdom and belief in our shared dreams have propelled us forward, even in the face of uncertainty. Your faith in my abilities has fueled my confidence and spurred me to achieve greater heights. Beyond the entrepreneurial sphere, and most importantly you have taught me invaluable life lessons. Your loyalty, respect, and patience have molded me into a better person. Your constant presence and support has provided me with a solid foundation from which to grow and thrive. Duane, I am forever grateful for your love, understanding, and belief in me. I'm so thankful of how God uses His breathe through you. Your boundless dedication to our family and our shared aspirations is nothing short of awe-inspiring. To my amazing husband, Duane, thank you for being my rock, my confidant, and my partner in all aspects of life. I am truly blessed to have you by my side, and I look forward to our continued journey together, building a future filled with love, success, and endless possibilities.

With loving gratitude, your Best Friend and Wife

Crystal

Contents

CH.1. INTRODUCTION DISCOVERING YOUR YES MOMENTS ...6

CH.2. THE TREASURE WITHIN - UNLEASH YOUR HIDDEN PO-
TENTIAL 9

CH.3. CONFIDENCE UNCHAINED - CONQUERING SELF-DOUBT
AND LIMITATIONS 12

CH.4. OWN IT - HOW ACCOUNTABILITY TRANSFORMS YOUR
LIFE 15

CH.5. FOSTERING A SUPPORTIVE COMMUNITY - YOUR TRIBE

....18

CH.6. BREAK THE CHAINS - CONQUER OBSTACLES AND
THRIVE 21

CH.7. THE PATH OF INFINITE POSSIBILITIES - CARVING YOUR
WAY TO TRIUMPH 24

CH.8. YOU ARE THE ANSWER - EMBRACE THE POWER WITHIN

....27

CH.9. CONNECTING THE DOTS - WEAVING THE TAPESTRY OF
GROWTH 30

CH.10. KEEP GOING - EMBRACING THE BOLD PATH AHEAD ...33

CH.11. EMBRACING CHANGE: THRIVING IN A DYNAMIC
WORLD 37

CH.12. NURTURING RESILIENCE: BOUNCING BACK STRONGER

....41

CH.13. THE POWER OF MINDSET: SHAPING YOUR REALITY ..45

CH.14. THE RIPPLE EFFECT: MAKING WAVES IN THE WORLD 49

CH.15. THE JOURNEY UNLEASHED: IGNITING LIMITLESS
GROWTH 52

Book Introduction

"Ellivate" is a transformative guidebook that aims to empower individuals to tap into their true potential and create a fulfilling and successful life. In this book, we will explore the key principles and strategies that will help you uncover your hidden talents, overcome self-doubt, and embrace a mindset of growth and abundance.

Chapter by Chapter Overview:

Chapter 1: Introduction - Discovering Your YES: Moments Embark on a personal journey to unlock your potential and discover the moments that ignite your passion and purpose, guiding you towards clarity and aspirations.

Chapter 2: The Treasure Within - Unleashing Your Hidden Potential: Uncover the hidden treasures and talents within you. Tap into your unique strengths and abilities to achieve remarkable success through self-reflection, practical techniques, and a deep exploration of your untapped potential.

Chapter 3: Confidence Unchained - Conquering Self-Doubt and Limitations: Break free from the chains of self-doubt and build unwavering confidence. Cultivate a positive mindset, embrace your worth, and gain the courage to overcome limitations, empowering yourself to reach new heights.

Chapter 4: Own It - How Accountability Transforms Your Life: Take ownership of your actions and choices for personal growth. Set meaningful goals, create action plans, and stay committed. Develop discipline and resilience, transforming your life into a journey of purpose and lasting success.

Chapter 5: Fostering a Supportive Community - Your Tribe: Build meaningful relationships and find your tribe, a network of individuals who uplift and inspire you. Experience personal and professional growth through a strong support system that fuels your journey and amplifies your impact.

Chapter 6: Break the Chains - Conquer Obstacles and Thrive: Navigate the obstacles faced by entrepreneurs with practical strategies. Overcome fear of failure, navigate uncertainty, and transform obstacles into opportunities that propel your business forward on the path to success.

Chapter 7: Path of Infinite Possibilities - Carving Your Way to Triumph: Discover the diverse pathways to success and develop a roadmap for your personal and professional journey. Identify opportunities, make informed decisions, and leverage your unique strengths to create a life that aligns with your vision of success.

Chapter 8: YOU Are the Answer - Embrace the Power Within: Emphasize self-belief and personal responsibility as the keys to unlocking your true potential. Harness the power within you to shape your destiny and create a life of fulfillment, knowing that you are the ultimate driver of your success.

Chapter 9: Connecting the Dots - Weaving the Tapestry of Growth: Reflect, recognize patterns, and align your actions with your values to gain valuable insights and set intentional goals. Navigate the journey of self-discovery and purposeful growth, making meaningful connections that contribute to your personal and professional development.

Chapter 10: Keep Going - Embracing the Bold Path Ahead: Reflect on your journey, set intentional goals, and embrace the path that lies ahead with courage, determination, and an unwavering belief in your potential. Recognize that personal and professional growth is a lifelong pursuit and commit to continuing the transformative journey beyond the pages of this book.

Chapter 11: Embracing Change: Explore the transformative power of change and embrace the mindset, resilience, and adaptability needed to navigate life's ever-changing landscape. Open yourself to new opportunities and possibilities for growth, cultivating resilience and creating a purposeful and evolving life.

Chapter 12: Nurturing Resilience - Bouncing Back Stronger: Cultivate resilience amidst adversity, unleashing your potential to conquer challenges and flourish. Develop the inner strength and fortitude to overcome obstacles, bounce back stronger, and reach new heights in your personal and professional journey.

Chapter 13: The Power of the Mindset - Shaping Your Reality: Cultivate a positive, growth-oriented mindset to overcome challenges, attract abundance, and shape a vibrant life. Harness the power of your thoughts, beliefs, and attitudes as you embark on a journey of personal transformation and create a reality filled with purpose and joy.

Chapter 14: The Ripple Effect - Making Waves in the World: Create a positive ripple effect through your actions and choices, making a profound difference in the world. Embrace kindness, live with purpose, and contribute to the greater good, leaving a legacy that transcends time and inspires others to

Chapter 15: The Journey Unleashed - Igniting Limitless Growth: Dive into the lifelong journey of growth and self-discovery. Embrace the power of lifelong learning, curiosity, and setting new goals. Let your life be a testament to the limitless possibilities that unfold when you commit to continuous self-improvement. Embrace the journey, fuel your passion, and let your extraordinary potential shine brightly. YOUR adventure awaits!

Chapter 1

Introduction Discovering Your YES Moments

Welcome to the exhilarating beginning of your transformative journey! Get ready to ignite your inner fire and unleash the power of your YES moments. In this chapter, we embark on a quest to uncover those electrifying instances in your life that scream "YES!" and set your soul on fire.

Think back to those heart-pounding moments when you felt unstoppable, when every cell in your body buzzed with excitement and purpose. Those are your YES moments, my friend, and they hold the key to unlocking your true potential. Together, we will dive deep into these exhilarating experiences and unravel the tapestry of passion and destiny they weave.

Through captivating exercises and thought-provoking prompts, we will peel back the layers of doubt and hesitation and unearth the brilliant gems that lie within you. Your YES moments are not mere flukes; they are divine sparks guiding you towards a life of fulfillment and authentic success.

Prepare yourself as we connect the dots and uncover the patterns that define your journey. These moments are your compass, pointing you towards a life that resonates with your deepest desires. Get ready to infuse your life with excitement, purpose, and limitless possibilities. The time to unleash your greatness is now!

In the chapters that follow, we will take an audacious leap into self-discovery, empowerment, and unstoppable growth. Embracing your YES moments will unlock doors you never thought possible. So, buckle up, dear reader, and get ready for a wild adventure that will transform your life forever.

Remember, you are the captain of your destiny. It's time to seize your YES moments, spread your wings, and soar to new heights of possibility and fulfillment. Your extraordinary life is waiting, and together, we will create a symphony of greatness that will echo through the ages.

Your Next 7 Steps

1.   Ignite the fire: Reflect on your past YES moments and relive the electrifying rush of joy, fulfillment, and alignment. Uncover the common threads that weave your tapestry of passion and purpose.

2.   Dare to dream: Set your intentions ablaze by defining clear and audacious goals for both your personal and professional life. Write them down and declare them to the universe with unwavering confidence.

3.   Embrace your inner bad ass: Adopt a fearless growth mindset and tackle challenges head-on. Embrace the power of resilience and believe in your limitless capacity to learn, adapt, and conquer.

4.   Rock your tribe: Surround yourself with the dreamers and believers who radiate positivity and uplift your spirits. Create a tribe that inspires, supports, and pushes you to reach for the stars.

5.   Unleash your power moves: Break down your goals into audacious action steps and unleash your unstoppable momentum. Embrace the thrill of progress and fearlessly charge ahead, leaving no room for doubt or hesitation.

6.   Fuel your inner fire: Embrace self-care as an act of rebellion against mediocrity. Nourish your mind, body, and soul with invigorating practices like exercise, mindfulness, and soul-stirring adventures.

7.   Gratitude with attitude: Embrace a mindset of gratitude, fiercely celebrating the present moment and the triumphs along your journey. Express gratitude for the challenges that shape you and savor every victory, no matter how small.

Get ready to embark on this audacious quest, my fellow adventurer. Embrace the extraordinary power of your YES moments and prepare to unleash the magnificent force that lies within you. Your destiny beckons, and together, we shall create a symphony of boldness, spunk, and unstoppable triumph. Let's rock this journey like the fearless warriors we are!

Chapter 2

The Treasure Within - Unleash Your Hidden Potential

Prepare to embark on a thrilling journey of self-discovery, where we'll dig deep and unleash the untamed power that resides within you. In this chapter, we'll excavate the hidden gems of your unique potential and set them free to shine brightly.

Picture a world where you fully embrace and unleash your extraordinary talents, skills, and abilities. It's time to bring that vision to life and step into your greatness. Release any doubts and limitations that have held you back, for you can achieve greatness beyond your wildest dreams.

Throughout this chapter, we'll dive headfirst into a series of introspective exercises designed to unlock your hidden potential. We'll explore your passions, interests, and natural talents, revealing the extraordinary qualities that define you. Embrace this process with unapologetic curiosity and an unyielding spirit, because within these explorations lies the true essence of your greatness.

By unleashing your hidden potential, you'll tap into a boundless wellspring of creativity, innovation, and brilliance. Prepare to be awestruck as you uncover strengths and abilities you never knew existed, or perhaps dismissed. These awe-inspiring revelations will ignite an inferno within you, propelling you towards your goals and dreams with unwavering determination.

As you unlock your hidden potential, moments of clarity and insight will illuminate your path. Eureka moments will guide you towards endeavors and pursuits that align perfectly with your true purpose. Embrace these electrifying moments with gratitude and enthusiasm, for they are the steppingstones on your journey to self-actualization.

Remember, dear reader, you are a unique force of nature, brimming with gifts and talents that are meant to dazzle the world. By unleashing your hidden potential, you not only enhance your own life but also ignite a wildfire of inspiration for those around you.

Embrace the adventure of self-discovery, for within it lies the keys to unlocking the treasures that await.

The time has come to unleash the full force of your hidden potential. Brace yourself for a transformational journey that will challenge, inspire, and ultimately mold you into a force to be reckoned with. As you step into your greatness, the world will bear witness to the remarkable impact you are destined to make that has awaited your attention. Embrace your hidden potential and prepare to forge a life of purpose, fulfillment, and audacious triumph. The time to unleash your greatness is now!

Get ready to embark on an extraordinary adventure of self-discovery, where you'll uncover the treasures within and awaken the dormant powers that have patiently been waiting.

Your Next 7 Steps

1.   Own your strengths: Uncover and celebrate your unique strengths, talents, and skills. Let them shine brightly as you maximize your potential.

2.   Dare to be bold: Break free from your comfort zone and embrace new experiences. Challenge the status quo and discover untapped potential that will leave you exhilarated.

3.   Embrace boundless learning: Commit to lifelong learning and personal development. Engage in voracious reading, attend awe-inspiring workshops, and seek mentors who push your boundaries and expand your horizons.

4.   Set audacious goals: Set goals that ignite your inner fire and push you beyond your current limits. Break them down into bite-sized milestones and relish the thrill of tracking your progress.

5.   Cultivate a growth mindset: Embrace a mindset of boundless growth and see failures as steppingstones towards your hidden potential. Welcome challenges as your allies in unleashing your greatness, and let resilience be your superpower.

6.   Seek guidance fearlessly: Embrace feedback from trusted mentors, coaches, and peers. Let constructive criticism be the fuel that propels your growth and improvement.

7.   Believe in your untamed power: Cultivate unwavering self-belief and confidence in your abilities. Banish self-doubt and embrace the unshakable trust that you possess the inner resources to unleash your hidden potential.

Are you ready to unleash the unruly force within you? Let's roar with boldness and spunk as we tap into your hidden potential and unleash your true power upon the world!

Chapter 3

Confidence Unchained - Conquering Self-Doubt and Limitations

Unleash the indomitable power that resides within your soul! In this exhilarating chapter, we embark on a transformative journey to annihilate self-doubt and demolish the limitations that have held you captive. It's time to unlock a life of audacious confidence and unshakable belief in your abilities.

Banish self-doubt from your mind and shatter the chains that bind you. No longer will you succumb to the whispers of uncertainty that undermine your potential. Embrace the audacity to break free and step into a realm where possibilities are limitless, and success is your birthright.

But remember, dear reader, confidence is not a privilege reserved for a chosen few—it's a skill that can be honed and mastered. It starts with a seismic shift in mindset—a shift from dwelling on potential failures to embracing the exhilarating potential for success.

It's about recognizing your intrinsic worth, celebrating your strengths, and embracing the unwavering belief that greatness flows through your veins.

Throughout this chapter, we'll arm you with practical strategies and exhilarating exercises to vanquish self-doubt and obliterate limitations. We'll dive deep into the roots of your insecurities, systematically dismantling them with unwavering courage and an unwavering belief in your potential. You'll discover that your doubts are mere illusions, easily shattered by your tenacity and unyielding faith in yourself.

As you journey through this chapter, brace yourself for extraordinary revelations and a surge of empowerment. Revel in the ah-ha moments that illuminate the boundless potential within you. The truths obscured by self-doubt will be revealed, and the dormant greatness that yearns to be unleashed will roar to life.

Embrace these transformative moments with unwavering certainty in your abilities.

Allow them to fuel your relentless determination and propel you towards astonishing heights. Remember, dear reader, you possess immeasurable capabilities far beyond what you currently perceive. It's time to dismantle the shackles of self-doubt and bask in the radiant glow of your own unwavering confidence.

With every step you take on this liberation journey, you'll forge an unbreakable spirit, resilient and fortified by newfound self- assurance. As the remnants of self-doubt crumble, a newfound freedom will engulf you—a freedom to pursue your wildest dreams, take audacious actions, and conquer the world with unwavering confidence.

Embrace this chapter as the catalyst for profound change—a change that empowers you to soar above your limitations and embrace a life characterized by unbridled confidence. The time has come to unchain your confidence and unleash the uncontainable force within. Brace yourself for an odyssey that will forever revolutionize your perception of self and propel you to the highest echelons of triumph. You are limitless, and your confidence knows no bounds.

Your Next 7 Steps

1.   Demolish negative self-talk: Recognize and annihilate the venomous whispers of negative self-talk. Replace them with empowering thoughts that fuel your growth and propel you towards greatness

2.   Exult in your victories: Celebrate every triumph, no matter how small, with unbridled enthusiasm. Cultivate a habit of acknowledging your strengths and savoring your accomplishments, amplifying your self-confidence.

3. **Embrace self-compassion:** Shower yourself with kindness and compassion. Treat yourself as the cherished friend you deserve, and engage in self-care practices that nurture your mind, body, and spirit.

4. **Surround yourself with champions:** Forge a tribe of champions who believe in your limitless potential. Surround yourself with mentors, peers, and allies who inspire confidence and fuel your relentless growth.

5. **Envision triumphant success:** Harness the power of visualization to vividly imagine yourself conquering your goals with unflinching confidence. Immerse yourself in the emotions of achievement and boldly claim your rightful success

6. **Embrace daring risks:** Venture outside your comfort zone and embrace calculated risks that challenge your perceived limitations. Embrace new opportunities and trust in your abilities to navigate uncharted territory.

7. **Master the art of assertiveness:** Hone your assertiveness skills to fearlessly express your thoughts, needs, and boundaries. Communicate with eloquence and conviction, advocating for yourself with unapologetic assertiveness and respect.

Now, dear reader, gather your audacity, fortify your spirit, and unleash the fiery phoenix of confidence within. The world awaits your unstoppable brilliance!

Chapter 4

Own It - How Accountability Transforms Your Life

Are you ready to ignite the flame of transformation within? In this electrifying chapter, we unleash the awe-inspiring impact of accountability on your life. Brace yourself for an empowering journey that will revolutionize your path to greatness and reshape your destiny.

Owning it means embracing the driving force behind your own existence. It's about seizing responsibility for your choices and their outcomes, regardless of their nature. By embracing accountability, you take the reins of your life, directing it with purpose and intention.

Throughout this chapter, we unveil the extraordinary nature of accountability. Discover how it empowers you to set audacious goals, take decisive action, and conquer any challenge that comes your way. Through accountability, you cultivate the discipline and resilience needed to transcend obstacles and achieve enduring success.

Accountability is not about finger-pointing or dwelling on past missteps; it's about gleaning wisdom from them and forging a path of growth. We explore practical strategies and tools that keep you focused, track your progress, and stoke the fires of commitment. Accountability becomes your mighty ally, a wellspring of empowerment and motivation.

As you journey through this chapter, be prepared for seismic shifts in your mindset and approach to life. Revel in those epiphany-filled moments that showcase the transformative might of owning your choices and actions. Realize that you hold the power to shape your destiny and manifest the life you crave.

Embrace these moments with unwavering boldness and unyielding determination.

Welcome the liberation that springs forth from taking charge of your growth and success. Remember, dear reader, you are not defined by your past; you are defined by the choices you make today and the actions you take tomorrow.

By embracing accountability, you unlock the gates to infinite possibilities. You become the master architect of your destiny, forging a path that aligns with your values, passions, and aspirations. Embrace the majestic power of ownership, for through accountability, you will metamorphose your life and leave an indelible mark on the world.

The time has come to seize your greatness, seize control of your journey, and embrace the boundless expanse of your potential. As you fully embrace accountability, witness the extraordinary transformation that unfurls within you. Prepare to be astonished by the heights you can attain when you truly own it. The power lies within your grasp.

Your Next 7 Steps

1.   Engrave your goals with unwavering clarity and deadlines: Set goals that resonate deeply and establish clear deadlines to hold yourself accountable. Break them down into actionable steps and track your progress with relentless determination.

2.   Forge an unyielding alliance: Seek an accountability partner or join a group of like-minded individuals who share your aspirations and values. Engage in regular check-ins, exchange progress reports, and ignite each other's spirits with unwavering support and motivation.

3.   Craft a measurement and tracking system: Design a robust system to monitor your progress and measure your results. Utilize calendars, habit trackers, or cutting-edge apps to hold yourself accountable and propel you forward.

4.   Command the realm of your actions: Embrace ownership of your choices and actions. Refuse to make excuses or cast blame on others. Recognize that you hold the power to shape your responses and make intentional decisions.

5.   Transmute setbacks into steppingstones: Embrace setbacks as opportunities for growth rather than failures. Dissect what went awry, adjust, and harness the experience to refine and elevate yourself.

6.   Celebrate milestones and conquests: Revel in the glory of your achievements along the journey. Celebrate each milestone reached and reward yourself for your unwavering dedication. This triumphant recognition fuels the fire of motivation, propelling you ever closer to your accountable destiny.

7.   Reflect and redefine: Regularly reflect on your progress and redefine your goals and strategies. Adapt your approach as needed to stay in perfect alignment with your vision and maintain unwavering accountability in your actions.

Now, dear reader, summon your audacity, infuse your spirit with unwavering vigor, and unleash the majestic power of accountability. The world awaits the marvels you shall achieve!

Chapter 5

Fostering a Supportive Community - Your Tribe

Prepare to embark on a thrilling expedition into the extraordinary realm of community. In this chapter, we unlock the secrets of fostering a supportive tribe that propels you to heights beyond your imagination. Brace yourself for a journey of connection, collaboration, and collective growth.

No individual achieves greatness in isolation. It is within the embrace of a like-minded tribe that true success flourishes. Your tribe consists of those who uplift, inspire, and ignite your fire. They believe in your dreams, celebrate your victories, and provide a sanctuary for growth and collaboration.

Together, we unravel the blueprint for building and nurturing your tribe. We delve into the power of networking, the essence of mentorship, and the profound value of authentic connections. Your tribe becomes your fortress—a place of support, guidance, and limitless inspiration.

As you journey through this chapter, a profound sense of gratitude will envelop you, fortifying your commitment to nurturing your tribe. Eureka moments will illuminate your path as you realize the immeasurable value of a supportive community. You will grasp that together, you can conquer mountains, forge new paths, and achieve far more than you ever could alone.

Embrace these moments with deep gratitude and a fierce determination to cultivate and nourish your tribe. Foster connections, offer unwavering support, and actively contribute to the growth of others. Remember, dear reader, your tribe is not just a pillar of support; it is a reciprocal relationship that elevates everyone involved.

By fostering a supportive community, you cultivate an ecosystem where dreams blossom, obstacles crumble, and triumphs are celebrated. Your tribe becomes the driving force behind your personal and professional growth, providing the encouragement and accountability needed to ascend to unprecedented heights.

The time has come to unleash the power of your tribe, to build relationships that fuel your journey to extraordinary success. Together, we embark on a magnificent adventure of connection, collaboration, and collective growth. Prepare to bask in the synergy of your tribe—a force that celebrates your victories and steadfastly supports you through any challenge.

Your Next 7 Steps

1. Ignite your values and passions: Unleash the brilliance of your values and passions, shaping the community you crave. Identify the qualities and values that resonate with your soul and attract those who align with your vision.

2. Seek kindred spirits: Embark on a quest to find like-minded individuals who share your interests, aspirations, and values. Seek out events, groups, and online communities where you can connect with those who ignite your soul.

3. Foster profound connections: Nurture genuine, meaningful relationships by investing time and effort in their cultivation. Embrace authenticity, support, and a sincere interest in others. Show up unapologetically as your true self, attracting those who appreciate and uplift you.

4. Be a pillar of support: Radiate unwavering support and encouragement to your tribe. Celebrate their victories, provide guidance when needed, and extend a helping hand. Cultivate a culture of support and collaboration, where growth is celebrated collectively.

5. Collaborate for boundless impact: Engage in collaborative projects or initiatives with fellow tribe members. Leverage each other's strengths and expertise to achieve shared goals and magnify your impact on the world.

6. **Cultivate constant communication:** Stay connected with your tribe through regular, open lines of communication. Embrace in person gatherings, virtual hangouts, vibrant group chats, or captivating newsletters. Foster an environment where transparent communication and collaboration thrive.

7. **Give abundantly to your tribe:** Contribute selflessly to the growth and well-being of your community. Volunteer your time, share your wisdom and skills, or initiate projects that amplify collective prosperity. Through active contribution, you forge unbreakable bonds within your tribe.

Now, dear reader, summon your audacity, infuse your spirit with unyielding vigor, and unleash the extraordinary power of your tribe. Together, you will illuminate the world with brilliance and leave an indelible mark upon the tapestry of existence. The time to embrace the force of your tribe is now. Let the thrilling journey begin!

Chapter 6

Break the Chains - Conquer Obstacles and Thrive

Prepare to unleash your inner warrior as we dive headfirst into the thrilling battlefield of entrepreneurship. In this chapter, we will shatter the chains that bind us and conquer every obstacle that stands in our path to business success. Get ready to embrace boldness, resilience, and unwavering determination like never before.

Running a business is not for the faint of heart. It demands unwavering courage, adaptability, and a fierce determination to overcome obstacles. As we embark on this chapter, prepare to dismantle the barriers that hinder your progress and transform them into launching pads for growth and innovation.

This chapter will be your weapon, forging a mindset of unyielding resilience and adaptability. Discover how to transform obstacles into springboards for growth and creativity. Unleash your strengths, pivot with agility, and turn setbacks into fuel for your unstoppable journey to success.

As you march through this chapter, prepare to be enlightened and invigorated. Aha moments will illuminate your path as you realize the dormant power within you to break free from the chains of adversity. Embrace the immense potential that lies within challenges, harnessing them as catalysts for your personal and professional metamorphosis.

Remember, dear reader, obstacles are not barriers but invitations to ascend higher.

Embrace them as steppingstones of opportunity, pushing you to learn, innovate, and evolve. Every obstacle you overcome fortifies your entrepreneurial spirit, equipping you with the skills and resilience needed to conquer the business world.

With each victorious battle, you lay the foundation of experience and wisdom. As you shatter the chains of limitation, new pathways to success reveal themselves. Embrace the challenges, adapt fearlessly, and forge ahead with unwavering determination.

The journey of entrepreneurship is not for the faint-hearted, but you possess the audacity and vision to overcome any obstacle that dares to cross your path. As you embrace this chapter, prepare to break free from the chains that bind you and emerge as a warrior entrepreneur, unstoppable in your pursuit of greatness.

The time has come to rise above challenges, to transform setbacks into triumphs, and to unleash your full potential as a business owner. Get ready to break the chains that confine you and pave the path of success, innovation, and impact. You possess the indomitable spirit to overcome any obstacle and triumph in your business. Let the battle begin!

Your Next 7 Steps

1.   **Ignite a warrior mindset:** Adopt a warrior mindset that sees challenges as opportunities for growth and conquest. Believe in your ability to overcome any obstacle and devise innovative solutions.

2.   **Identify and dismantle obstacles:** Fearlessly identify and dismantle the obstacles in your path. Analyze their origins and potential impact on your business. Prepare to conquer them one.by one.

3.   **Craft a strategic battle plan:** Forge a strategic battle plan to overcome each obstacle. Break it down into tactical steps, setting clear goals and deadlines. Prioritize the most formidable challenges and allocate resources wisely.

4.   **Seek wisdom and camaraderie:** Rally support from mentors, coaches, and industry veterans. Their wisdom and camaraderie will provide invaluable guidance as you navigate through obstacles. Never underestimate the strength that comes from a united front.

5.   **Embrace unyielding resilience:** Cultivate unwavering resilience by seeing setbacks as steppingstones to success. Learn from

failures, rebound swiftly, and adapt to change with unbreakable determination. You are a warrior destined for victory.

6.   Seize calculated opportunities: Fearlessly seize calculated opportunities to conquer obstacles. Assess the risks and rewards, make informed decisions, and charge forward with unwavering confidence. Embrace innovation and unconventional solutions.

7.   Stay unrelentingly focused: Maintain laser-sharp focus on your goals and relentlessly pursue them. Obstacles may arise, but they will never extinguish your unwavering determination. Persevere fiercely, adjust strategies as needed, and keep your vision burning bright.

Get ready to unleash your warrior spirit, conquer all obstacles, and emerge triumphant in the battlefield of business. The journey ahead is not for the weak-hearted, but you possess the audacity and resolve to claim victory. Charge forward fearlessly, for success awaits those who dare to break the chains!

Chapter 7

The Path of Infinite Possibilities - Carving Your Way to Triumph

Welcome to the chapter that sets your journey ablaze with audacious ambition and unwavering tenacity. Here, we unravel the intricate tapestry of opportunities that pave the way to triumph. Prepare to unleash your inner adventure as we navigate through the boundless realm of possibilities, forging a path that leads to your greatest aspirations.

Opportunities abound, but it is your keen perception and bold action that transforms them into life-altering moments. In this chapter, we dive deep into the art of recognizing, seizing, and capitalizing on opportunities. By honing your awareness and embracing a fearless mindset, you will unravel a treasure trove of possibilities that align perfectly with your passions, talents, and dreams.

We embark on a riveting exploration of diverse opportunity pathways, be it in the realm of business, career, or personal growth. Tales of those who have navigated these paths will leave you breathless, igniting your imagination and expanding the horizons of what you believe is attainable. Let their journeys become the catalyst that propels you forward, armed with inspiration and fortified by their triumphs.

As we journey together, prepare to ignite your intuition and cultivate the ability to discern opportunities even in the most unexpected of places. Embrace the audacious mindset of curiosity and endless potential, for within its embrace lies the secret to uncovering hidden gems that others overlook. Embrace the uncertainty, embrace calculated risks, for behind every opportunity lies the potential for immense growth and immeasurable rewards.

In moments of profound revelation, the dots will connect, revealing the interconnectedness of seemingly unrelated events and experiences.

Clarity will emerge, guiding you towards the opportunities that align with your values and propel you towards your long-term aspirations. These flashes of insight will become your guiding stars as you traverse the expansive landscape of possibilities.

Always remember, dear reader, that opportunities are not mere chance encounters, but pathways that lead to a life of fulfillment and triumph. Embrace them as keys that unlock new experiences, connections, and achievements. Each opportunity seized becomes a steppingstone on your remarkable journey to greatness.

As you progress through this chapter, cultivate a mindset of abundance, recognizing that opportunities are limitless and within your grasp. Develop the confidence to step outside your comfort zone, embrace unfamiliar challenges, and trust in your ability to navigate the ever-changing terrain of opportunity.

The time has come to embark on an odyssey of discovery and expansion. With unwavering determination, an open heart, and a razor-sharp eye, navigate the labyrinthine pathways of opportunity. Embrace the limitless possibilities that lie before you, for you possess the power to shape your destiny by fearlessly seizing the opportunities that present themselves.

Let this chapter serve as your compass, equipping you with wisdom and insights to navigate the intricate web of possibilities that await. Embrace the adventure, embrace the unknown, and embark upon the extraordinary journey that leads you to the success and fulfillment your heart desires. The world brims with opportunity—embrace it with unbridled enthusiasm and forge ahead on your transformative quest for greatness.

Your Next 7 Steps

1.   **Envision your triumph:** Craft a vivid vision of your ultimate success, leaving no detail unimagined. Let this vision guide you to the opportunities that align with your deepest desires.

2.   Embrace the seeker's mindset: Embody the spirit of an audacious seeker, always on the lookout for hidden opportunities. Maintain an insatiable curiosity and an openness to new possibilities.

3.   Assess risks with fearlessness: Fearlessly evaluate the risks and rewards of each opportunity. Consider their potential impact on your personal and professional life, aligning them with your values and aspirations.

4.   Set the course with strategic goals: Chart your path by setting strategic goals that lead you toward the opportunities you wish to seize. Break them down into actionable steps and create a roadmap for achievement.

5.   Cultivate the growth warrior within: Nurture the spirit of a growth warrior, perceiving challenges as opportunities for growth and unwaveringly believing in your capacity to learn and adapt. Embrace novelty and calculate risks.

6.   Forge connections, ignite alliances: Forge powerful connections with kindred spirits who can support and propel you towards opportunities. Immerse yourself in industry events, professional networks, and engaging communities.

7.   Boldly conquer, seize the day: Once an opportunity has been assessed and your strategic plan is in place, take bold, decisive action. Banish hesitation and fear, embracing the opportunities that come your way with unwavering confidence and relentless determination.

Embrace these action steps as a clarion call to transformative change, ignited with audacity and imbued with unyielding commitment. Let them be the catalysts that propel you towards a future adorned with growth, resounding triumphs, and boundless fulfillment. The journey ahead holds infinite promise—embrace it with unwavering courage and set forth on the path to extraordinary triumph!

Chapter 8

YOU are the Answer - Embrace the Power Within

Prepare to witness the birth of a cosmic force as we delve into the heart of your true potential. In this chapter, we plunge into the depths of your being, igniting the flame that illuminates your path to greatness. Brace yourself for a thrilling exploration of self-discovery, where you unleash the dynamic force that resides within you.

Gone are the days of seeking external validation and guidance, for the truth you've been yearning for lies deep within your own essence. YOU possess an extraordinary fusion of talents, wisdom, and intuition that, when unleashed and embraced, propels you towards the realization of your wildest dreams.

Embrace this chapter as your portal to self-empowerment and transformation. Together, we shall venture forth, unraveling the importance of self-belief, self-acceptance, and self-compassion. By embracing your authentic self and recognizing your inherent worth, you unleash an unstoppable reservoir of creativity, confidence, and resilience.

Prepare for a mind-altering journey as we peel back the layers that have obscured your true radiance. Within the depths of your soul, we shall unearth the passions that set your spirit ablaze, the values that serve as your guiding light, and the unique perspectives that shape the tapestry of your existence. Embrace this sacred opportunity to rediscover and reconnect with the extraordinary being that you are.

As you traverse this chapter, be prepared for earth-shattering revelations and moments of profound self-awareness. Ah-ha moments shall pierce through the veil of illusion, illuminating the boundless power you possess to shape your reality. You are the revered author of your own narrative, and your potential knows no bounds.

Embrace these transformative moments with a fervent love and appreciation for your essence. Celebrate your strengths, dance with your quirks, and honor every step of your journey. Remember, you are an ever-evolving masterpiece, constantly unfolding and expanding. Trust in the wellspring of wisdom within, for it knows the path that leads to your highest good.

With each stride on this sacred voyage of self-discovery, you shall uncover the answers you seek. Trust in the symphony of your intuition and listen closely to the whispers of your heart. Believe that within you lies the profound knowledge, unwavering courage, and boundless resilience needed to conquer any obstacle and create a life of purpose and fulfillment.

Dear reader, within the depths of your being lies the answer you've been yearning for. Embrace your unique gifts, follow the symphony of your passions, and trust in the extraordinary potential that resides within you. The world hungers for your unique voice, your unparalleled contributions. Embrace your inner powerhouse and let it radiate with an intensity that ignites the spirits of others.

The time has come to recognize that the answers you seek are not distant echoes, but a resounding chorus resonating within your very core. Embrace the resplendent truth of your own magnificence and step into your role as the answer to your own questions. With unwavering self-belief, you shall unleash a life brimming with infinite possibilities, leaving an indelible impact on the world around you. Embrace your power, embrace your truth, and let your brilliance shine with an intensity that dazzles the cosmos.

Your Next 7 Steps

1.   **Embrace the brilliance of self-reflection:** Immerse yourself in dedicated moments of self-reflection, plunging into the depths of your being to uncover the brilliance within. Unveil your strengths, passions, and values, discovering the patterns that shape your journey.

2.   **Seize the reins of your destiny:** Embrace the truth that you hold the key to shaping your life through the choices you make. Take

ownership of your decisions and their consequences, realizing that you are the maestro of your own success and happiness.

3.   Indulge in self-care extravaganzas: Make self-care an extravagant ritual, treating your physical, mental, and emotional

well-being as sacred treasures. Nourish your soul with exercise, mindfulness, and self-compassion, honoring the vessel that carries your magnificence.

4.   Cultivate an unshakable self-belief: Develop an unyielding self-belief in your boundless abilities and worth. Banish self- doubt, replacing it with unshakable confidence and an awe-inspiring self-image. Trust in your power and your unwavering capacity to surmount challenges and achieve your deepest desires.

5.   Establish a fortress of boundaries: Erect impenetrable boundaries to safeguard your time, energy, and well-being. Master the art of saying no to commitments and activities that fail to align with your priorities. By setting boundaries, you create a sacred space for what truly resonates with your soul.

6.   Embark on an odyssey of personal growth: Embark on an exhilarating odyssey of lifelong learning and personal growth. Seek out opportunities to expand your knowledge, acquire new skills, and amplify your strengths. Embrace personal development as a never-ending symphony.

7.   Revel in the splendor of your uniqueness: Embrace the majestic tapestry of your uniqueness, basking in its resplendent glory. Celebrate the qualities, perspectives, and experiences that set you apart. Embrace authenticity, allowing your true essence to radiate brightly, illuminating the path for others to do the same.

These steps, infused with audacity and spunk, have the potential to unlock a seismic transformation within your very being. Embrace them as catalysts for unparalleled metamorphosis, propelling you towards a future adorned with breathtaking growth, monumental triumphs, and unbounded fulfillment. Embrace your brilliance, let it soar, and revel in the magnificent masterpiece that is YOU.

Chapter 9

Connecting the Dots - Weaving the Tapestry of Growth

Life is an exhilarating tapestry, intricately woven with the threads of your experiences, lessons, and connections. In this chapter, prepare to embark on an audacious voyage of self-discovery and expansion as we fearlessly connect the dots of your personal and professional growth. Brace yourself for a transformational journey where the hidden patterns of wisdom reveal themselves, igniting the fire within.

Every moment, big or small, carries profound significance and serves as a steppingstone on your path. As we plunge into this chapter, we shall immerse ourselves in deep reflection, unraveling the pivotal moments, extracting the priceless lessons, and weaving together the rich tapestry of your journey. By connecting these dots, you unlock the power to navigate your future with intention and purpose.

Through immersive exercises and thought-provoking prompts, we shall delve into the core themes and recurring patterns that have shaped your life. We shall uncover the transformative growth opportunities and profound wisdom that lie within your personal and professional development. This empowering process of connecting the dots will illuminate the narrative that has propelled you forward, empowering you to make intentional choices that align with your truest desires.

As you navigate this chapter, embrace the exhilarating revelations that await. Ah-ha moments will burst forth as you connect seemingly unrelated events, witnessing the tapestry of your life weave into a breathtaking masterpiece. These moments of clarity will become your compass, illuminating the path towards aligned choices and seizing the boundless opportunities that beckon.

Embrace these moments with unyielding gratitude and an open heart. Each dot you connect brings you closer to unraveling the intricate wisdom that resides within your journey. Trust in the symphony of insights that emerges as you connect the dots and allow it to guide you towards a future overflowing with fulfillment, joy, and exponential personal and professional growth.

Dear reader, you are the master weaver of your own tapestry. Through connecting the dots of your experiences, you gain profound clarity about who you are, where you have been, and where your magnificent potential shall lead you. Embrace the journey of self-discovery, for it is within the interconnectedness of your life's experiences that you shall find boundless inspiration and guidance.

The time has come to boldly connect the dots, unravel the tapestry, and unearth the precious treasures of wisdom and growth within your journey. Get ready to embrace the transformative power of self-reflection and introspection. With each dot you connect, you shall stride towards a life imbued with purpose, alignment, and limitless possibilities. Let the discovery points of your personal and professional growth illuminate your path and lead you towards a future where you unleash your fullest potential.

Your Next 7 Steps

1.   Immerse in the brilliance of pivotal moments: Dive deep into the brilliance of significant moments that have shaped your being. Reflect on the threads that connect them, extract the timeless lessons, and unveil the growth opportunities that lie within

2.   Embrace the kaleidoscope of recurring patterns: Embrace the kaleidoscope of recurring patterns in your life, both triumphant and challenging. Recognize the symphony of themes that reverberate, and allow them to inform your future choices and actions

3.   Dare to defy perspectives: Courageously step beyond the boundaries of comfort and embrace new perspectives. Engage in conversations with diverse souls, absorbing their stories and insights.

Witness how this audacious exploration broadens your horizons and ignites your creativity.

4.   Indulge in a feast of knowledge: Feast upon the banquet of continuous learning and curiosity. Immerse yourself in self- study, devour books that expand your mind, participate in immersive workshops, and seek wisdom from awe-inspiring mentors. Commit to an unrelenting journey of personal and professional growth.

5.   Align with the symphony of values: Clarify the symphony of your core values, allowing them to serve as a compass for your actions and decisions. Harmonize your personal and professional life, living authentically and with unwavering purpose.

6.   Embrace the holistic crescendo: Embrace the symphony of holistic growth, recognizing that personal and professional realms intertwine harmoniously. Strive for equilibrium and unity, nurturing every facet of your being as you navigate this grand symphony of life.

7.   Paint your masterpiece with intention: Based on the dazzling insights gained from connecting the dots of your life, paint your masterpiece with intention. Set audacious goals that align with your vision and values. Fashion a roadmap for your personal and professional growth, marked by milestones and infused with actionable steps that propel you towards your highest aspirations.

Incorporate these steps with audacity and vibrancy, for they possess the power to manifest profound change in your existence. Embrace them as the keys that unlock the doors to unparalleled growth, extraordinary accomplishments, and an awe-inspiring future. Embrace your brilliance and allow the interconnected threads of your life to weave a tapestry of infinite possibility.

Chapter 10

Keep Going - Embracing the Bold Path Ahead

It's time to reflect upon the profound insights, empowering lessons, and transformative moments that have molded your path thus far. In this chapter, we dare to explore the path that lies ahead, igniting the flames of your personal and professional growth.

Prepare to embrace the audacious steps you can take to continue your extraordinary journey. Throughout this book, we fearlessly delved into the depths of self-discovery, unearthing our hidden potential, conquering self-doubt, harnessing the power of accountability, fostering supportive communities, overcoming obstacles, recognizing opportunities, and weaving the threads of our lives into a captivating tapestry. It has been a journey of empowerment, awakening, and remarkable transformation. Now, as you stand at this exhilarating crossroads, armed with newfound knowledge and self-awareness, it's time to chart an extraordinary course. This is your moment to define your goals with unwavering conviction, set intentions that resonate with your soul, and boldly seize the life you desire. The possibilities before you are limitless, and the power to shape your destiny rests firmly in your hands. In this chapter, we will explore dynamic strategies to fuel your growth and propel you forward on your journey toward unparalleled success and fulfillment.

We will delve into the significance of continuous learning, personal development, and unwavering alignment with your core values and purpose. By nurturing these vital aspects, you will flourish on an unceasing path of expansion and evolution. As you navigate the path ahead, fully embrace the profound lessons and insights gained from your courageous expedition.

Trust in the magnificent gifts that reside within you. Stay unwaveringly committed to your vision, allowing the dreams that ignite your soul to guide your every action. Let the wisdom you have acquired fuel your relentless pursuit of new horizons and breathtaking achievements.

Prepare for the exhilarating "ah-ha" moments that will continue to grace your journey.

Embrace them as powerful reminders of your infinite potential and the boundless possibilities that eagerly await your embrace. Open yourself to the unexpected, for it is often within the uncharted territory that the most remarkable growth unfolds, and where stepping beyond your comfort zone yields extraordinary rewards.

Your Next 7 Steps

1.   **Stay committed to growth:** Commit to a lifelong journey of growth and self-discovery. Embrace the mindset of a continuous learner, always seeking new opportunities for personal and professional development.

2.   **Review and refine your goals:** Regularly review and refine your goals to ensure they remain aligned with your evolving aspirations and values. Adjust as needed to stay on the path towards your desired future.

3.   **Cultivate resilience:** Embrace challenges as opportunities for growth and build resilience in the face of adversity. Develop the mindset and skills to bounce back from setbacks, learn from them, and keep moving forward

4.   **Foster a growth mindset:** Nurture a growth mindset that sees failures as learning experiences and believes in your ability to improve and evolve. Embrace a mindset that welcomes challenges and views them as steppingstones to success.

5.   **Seek meaningful connections:** Surround yourself with a supportive network of individuals who uplift and inspire you. Seek meaningful connections with like-minded individuals who share your values and goals. Collaborate, learn from one another, and support each other's growth.

6.   Take inspired action: Turn your dreams and aspirations into reality by taking inspired action. Break down your goals into actionable steps and consistently move forward. Embrace the discomfort of stepping outside your comfort zone and take bold leaps towards your vision.

7.   Embrace gratitude and celebrate progress: Cultivate gratitude for the journey and celebrate every step of progress along the way. Acknowledge and appreciate your accomplishments, no matter how big or small. Embracing gratitude keeps you grounded, motivated, and focused on the positive aspects of your journey.

Never forget, dear reader, that the journey of personal and professional growth is not merely a destination—it is an ongoing, exhilarating process. Embrace the mindset of a lifelong explorer, for there is an abundance of knowledge, experiences, and accomplishments awaiting your discovery. Although challenges may arise along the way, with each step, you become more resilient, more empowered, and one step closer to the realization of your most cherished dreams. As you draw near to the conclusion of this book, carry the radiant wisdom, transformative insights, and invigorating inspiration gained on this remarkable journey with you. Allow them to be the unwavering compass that guides you towards a life of profound purpose, enduring fulfillment, and extraordinary triumphs.

You possess the power to create a life that aligns with your deepest desires and to make an indelible impact on the world around you. The time has come to embark upon the path ahead with unyielding courage, unwavering determination, and an unwavering belief in your own brilliance. Embrace the challenges as catalysts for your growth, the setbacks as invaluable lessons, and the victories as triumphant milestones along your transformative odyssey. Your journey is unique, and the world eagerly awaits the remarkable impact you are destined to

make.

Dear reader, it is time to propel yourself forward on this thrilling expedition of self-discovery, relentless growth, and extraordinary success. The path that lies ahead gleams with infinite possibilities.

Embrace the adventure with unwavering trust in your own power and let the radiance of your brilliance shine brightly for all to see. You are capable of extraordinary things, and the path ahead is yours to illuminate and conquer. Go forth, dear reader, and fearlessly forge your destiny.

Continue your journey of extraordinary discovery, unstoppable growth, and awe-inspiring triumphs. The path ahead glimmers with boundless possibilities. Embrace the wild excitement, trust in your indomitable power, and let your light blaze a trail for others to follow. You are destined for greatness, and the world awaits the remarkable legacy you will create. This is your time. This is your journey. Make it a dazzling masterpiece of unbridled audacity.

Chapter 11

Embracing Change: Thriving in a Dynamic World

Change is the exhilarating dance of life. In this chapter, we embark on a thrilling exploration of mastering change and thriving in a dynamic world. Get ready to unleash your unyielding mindset, indomitable resilience, and relentless adaptability to conquer the ever-evolving landscape of life and business.

As we delve into this chapter, we unravel the essence of change and its profound impact on our personal and professional realms. We fearlessly confront the whirlwind of emotions and resistance that often accompany change, discovering invincible strategies to triumph over them. By embracing change, you unveil a tapestry of extraordinary opportunities and boundless possibilities for growth.

Change is a fertile ground for metamorphosis, both in our personal and professional lives. We delve deep into the secrets of cultivating flexibility, adaptability, and an insatiable growth mindset. Embrace the truth that change is not a foe but a catalyst for unparalleled innovation, profound learning, and magnificent evolution. As you gracefully adapt to change, you position yourself as an unstoppable force of unyielding triumph in an ever-changing world.

As you traverse the chapters of this enlightening journey, be unyielding in your pursuit of transformative change. Revel in the breathtaking moments of revelation as you shift your perspective, uncovering the hidden treasures and invaluable lessons that accompany each new phase of life. Embrace these moments with an unquenchable thirst for curiosity and an infectious thrill, for change is the catalyst that propels us towards infinite growth and relentless progress.

Beloved reader, change is not a specter to be feared but an ally to be embraced. It is the vital force that propels us ever forward, challenging us to transcend our limits and scale new heights. By embracing change with unyielding fervor, you wield the power to mold your destiny and forge a life that resonates with your deepest aspirations and unwavering values.

The time has come to cast aside the shackles of change-aversion and boldly step into the unknown abyss. Embrace the exhilarating trials and enigmatic uncertainties that accompany change, for they are the very steppingstones that pave the way to greatness. With each encounter with change, remember that within your indomitable spirit lies the power to adapt, flourish, and thrive.

Embracing change is not for the faint-hearted, but the rewards it begets are immeasurable. As you navigate the ever-shifting tides of the dynamic world, be an unwavering seeker of new perspectives, an intrepid champion of innovation, and a tireless advocate for continuous growth. Trust in your resolute ability to adapt swiftly and seize the magnificent opportunities that arise in the wake of change.

With each stride you take in embracing change, you fortify your resilience, broaden your horizons, and craft a life that is in perpetual motion—a life brimming with purpose, audacity, and profound metamorphosis. Embrace the riveting odyssey that awaits, dear reader, and let change be the zephyr that propels you ever forward towards an iridescent future of boundless possibilities.

Embrace the limitless power of adaptability: Embody the essence of change and embrace a mindset of invincible adaptability. Cultivate the unparalleled ability to recalibrate your plans, revitalize your perspectives, and redefine your strategies as circumstances unfold.

Your Next 7 Steps

1.   **Dance with discomfort and flourish in its wake:** Embrace the exhilarating embrace of growth that often lies beyond your comfort zone. Forge an unbreakable alliance with discomfort, knowing it serves

as the extraordinary catalyst for your personal and professional transformation.

2.   Unearth the treasures hidden within change: Discern the treasures that lie within the very heart of change. Rather than cowering in fear or resistance, train your spirit to unveil the astounding benefits and boundless possibilities that emerge. Embrace change as the gateway to remarkable experiences, boundless wisdom, and resplendent growth.

3.   Foster an unyielding spirit of resilience: Strengthen the sinews of your resilience to navigate the tempestuous seas that change may bring. Cultivate the invaluable coping mechanisms, embrace selfcare practices, and nurture a robust support system that fuels your indomitable spirit, allowing you to soar beyond setbacks and seamlessly adapt to new circumstances, relentlessly pursuing personal and professional development opportunities. Embrace change as a beckoning call to expand your skills, broaden your knowledge, and shatter the boundaries of your perspectives.

4.   Embark on an unrelenting quest for growth and evolution: Immerse yourself in the intoxicating realm of unyielding growth and evolution. Embrace a mindset that pulsates with insatiable curiosity, forever thirsting for new knowledge.

5.   Unleash the audacity of innovation and creativity: Embrace change as the sacred crucible of innovation and a fervent muse for creativity. Champion bold ideas, fervently embrace cutting-edge technologies, and fervently explore novel approaches that shall propel you ever higher. Embrace change as an electrifying invitation to experiment, iterate, and trailblaze unprecedented solutions.

6.   Master the art of mindful self-reflection: Cultivate the radiant aura of mindfulness and introspection to gracefully navigate change with utmost poise and unyielding self-awareness. Regularly embark on soul-searching expeditions, keenly observe the ebb and flow of your thoughts and emotions and adapt your mindset as the winds of change dictate.

7.   **Employ this introspection as a sacred** compass to guide your responses to change, ensuring they resonate harmoniously with your deepest values and audacious ambitions.

With these audacious and spirited steps, you unleash the tempestuous force of your potential. Embrace the transformative power of change and make an unwavering commitment to journey forward with relentless courage and unyielding audacity. The dynamic world shall tremble in awe as you harness the winds of change to sculpt your destiny, forging a future that transcends the boundaries of the imaginable.

Chapter 12

Nurturing Resilience: Bouncing Back Stronger

Resilience is the invincible superpower that propels us to rise triumphantly in the face of adversity. In this electrifying chapter, we unlock the art of nurturing resilience and unleash the indomitable strength within to conquer challenges and setbacks.

Get ready to wield the keys that unlock your true potential and soar to new heights.

Life's roller coaster is filled with exhilarating highs and daunting lows, but it is our response that truly defines us. Resilience is not about sidestepping difficulties; it's about fearlessly confronting them head-on, extracting invaluable wisdom, and emerging from the crucible stronger than ever before. It's the audacious ability to adapt, recover, and flourish amidst the storm.

In this awe-inspiring chapter, we journey into the realm of resilience, unraveling its mindset and transformative practices. We fearlessly traverse the power of positive thinking, the sacred embrace of self-compassion, and the relentless cultivation of a growth mindset. Through practical strategies and invigorating exercises, you will forge an arsenal of tools to navigate life's tempestuous challenges with grace, fortitude, and unyielding tenacity.

As you venture through this chapter, be prepared for electrifying moments of self-reflection and self-discovery. Revel in the exhilarating epiphanies that arise as you acknowledge your innate resilience and recognize that setbacks are not roadblocks, but gateways to unparalleled growth. Embrace these moments with fervent gratitude and an unwavering sense of empowerment, for within you lies the extraordinary capacity to bounce back, transcend limitations, and soar to unprecedented heights.

Dear reader, your resilience knows no bounds. Within the depths of your being, a wellspring of strength, courage, and determination awaits your embrace. By nurturing resilience, you unleash the boundless ability to face challenges head-on, maintain an unwavering positive outlook, and emerge victorious in the face of adversity.

The time has come to nurture your resilience and rise above every obstacle that dares to impede your path. Embrace the invaluable lessons that setbacks impart, viewing them as steppingstones that propel you towards the pinnacle of success. Trust unwaveringly in your ability to overcome, adapt, and emerge from the crucible of challenges stronger, wiser, and more resilient than ever before.

With each challenge that crosses your path, remember that you possess the invincible power to transcend it. Nurture your resilience through the sacred practices of self-care, the steadfast embrace of mindfulness, and the unwavering support of your tribe. Cultivate a mindset of unwavering growth and limitless possibility, recognizing that every setback is an extraordinary opportunity for unparalleled personal and professional development.

As you author the captivating chapters of your life, let resilience illuminate your path. Embrace challenges as transformative catalysts, learn from them, and allow them to propel you towards your true potential. Your unwavering resilience shall radiate as a beacon of hope, inspiring others to rise above their own obstacles and unapologetically embrace the boundless power that lies within them.

Your Next 7 Steps

1. **Cultivate a dauntless growth mindset:** Unleash the indomitable force of a growth mindset that sees challenges as thrilling opportunities for growth. Embrace setbacks as fleeting blips on the journey to triumph. Believe unwaveringly in your ability to learn, adapt, and surge forward stronger than ever before.

2. **Forge an unbreakable support network**: Surround yourself with an unwavering network of champions, be they family, friends, mentors, or support groups. Seek guidance, encouragement, and

unwavering empathy from those who kindle the fire within you during life's darkest moments.

3.   Indulge in relentless self-care: Prioritize self-care as the sacred oasis that nurtures your physical, mental, and emotional well-being. Engage in activities that invigorate your soul - be it vigorous exercise, serene mindfulness, soul-stirring hobbies, or quality time with cherished loved ones. Guard your well-being fiercely, for it is the bedrock of your resilience.

4.   Master the art of creative problem-solving: Hone your problem-solving prowess to deftly navigate challenges. Dissect problems into bite-sized fragments, unleash torrents of creativity to craft ingenious solutions, and embark on resolute action to surmount the hurdles that obstruct your path.

5.   Embrace the luminance of optimism and gratitude: Cultivate a resplendent mindset that pulsates with unwavering optimism and boundless gratitude. Train your gaze on the limitless opportunities and bountiful blessings that reside within every chapter of your life, even amidst the tempestuous winds of adversity.

6.   Embrace the boundless wisdom of setbacks: Revel in setbacks as invaluable mentors on the path of personal growth. Absorb the lessons and insights offered by these formidable teachers, harnessing their profound wisdom to inform your future decisions and actions. Failure morphs from a menacing roadblock into an illuminating steppingstone on your path to unparalleled growth.

7.   Harness the nimble spirit of adaptability: Cultivate the agile spirit of adaptability, gracefully pirouetting amidst the winds of change. Embrace the unknown with open arms, ceaselessly seeking opportunities to pivot and refine your plans. The more you embrace the exquisite dance of adaptability, the more your resilience soars to awe-inspiring heights.

With these audacious and spirited steps, you summon forth the unassailable fortress of your resilience. Embrace the transformative power that resides within you, as you unflinchingly traverse the journey towards unbounded triumph. The world shall tremble in awe as you conquer obstacles, unleash your limitless potential, and author an extraordinary future that defies all boundaries.

Chapter 13

The Power of Mindset: Shaping Your Reality

Within the vast cosmos of possibilities, your mindset reigns as the master architect of your reality. In this electrifying chapter, we plunge into the transformative depths of mindset and unlock the extraordinary potential that lies within your mind. Brace yourself to unleash the audacious force that shapes your world according to your deepest desires.

Your mindset is the omnipotent lens through which you perceive the universe and navigate the labyrinth of experiences. It determines the course you chart when faced with challenges, the way you seize opportunities, and the trajectory of your journey through life's myriad peaks and valleys. By harnessing the raw power of your mindset, you transcend limitations and breathe life into your dreams.

In this paradigm-shifting chapter, we embark on an expedition to explore the profound influence of mindsets on personal and professional growth. We dive headfirst into the boundless realms of the growth mindset, abundance mindset, and the awe-inspiring power of positive thinking. Armed with practical techniques and invigorating exercises, you shall forge a mindset that empowers you to surmount obstacles with unwavering resolve, embrace opportunities with audacious fervor, and manifest a life brimming with unparalleled fulfillment.

As you traverse the uncharted terrain of this chapter, embrace the audacity to challenge your existing beliefs and daringly embrace new perspectives. Revel in the illuminating "ah-ha" moments that emerge as you grasp the profound influence of your mindset on the intricate tapestry of your thoughts, emotions, and actions. Embrace these moments with unyielding confidence and an unshakable commitment to shaping your reality through the indomitable power of your mind.

Dear reader, you possess the majestic power to shape your reality through the formidable might of your mindset. By cultivating a luminous, growth-oriented mindset, you forge an unbreakable armor that enables you to surmount challenges, magnetize abundance, and sculpt a reality that aligns harmoniously with your most fervent desires.

Now is the time to relinquish the shackles of limiting beliefs and embrace the untapped reservoir of infinite possibilities that reside within your mind. Seize dominion over your thoughts, beliefs, and self-talk. Select empowering thoughts and affirmations that fuel your growth and reverberate in harmonious resonance with your vision of unparalleled success. By doing so, you create a fertile ground from which your dreams shall blossom and flourish.

With each sunrise, grasp the extraordinary power of your mindset and the reverberating influence it exerts over the canvas of your reality. Nourish a mindset that radiates with boundless possibility, unwavering resilience, and an ardent embrace of gratitude. Trust in the transcendental power of your thoughts to mold your experiences and summon forth a vibrant, purposeful existence teeming with resplendent joy.

Remember, dear reader, that you are the master of your reality through the invincible power of your mindset. Embrace the transformative nature of your thoughts, beliefs, and attitudes. Allow your mindset to guide you relentlessly towards your dreams and empower you to sculpt a life overflowing with abundance, fulfillment, and extraordinary achievements.

Your Next 7 Steps

1. **Ignite a wildfire of positivity:** Embrace the luminescent force of positive thinking and ignite a wildfire of radiant possibilities within your mind. Train your thoughts to unveil opportunities and untapped potential in every circumstance, propelling you towards a mindset brimming with abundance and perpetual growth.

2. **Obliterate the shackles of limiting beliefs:** Identify and obliterate the shackles of limiting beliefs that hinder your progress.

Examine the beliefs that erode your confidence, replacing them with invigorating convictions that fuel your unbridled growth and unwavering success.

3.   Forge an unyielding arsenal of affirmations: Harness the elemental power of affirmations to rewire the depths of your subconscious mind. Unleash a cascade of affirmations that harmonize with the reality you seek to create, steadfastly believing in their truth and unwaveringly embodying their wisdom.

4.   Bask in the luminosity of positive influences: Immerse yourself in the radiance of positive influences, be it illuminating books, captivating podcasts, or revered mentors who kindle the flames of inspiration within your soul. Opt to surround yourself with those who exude positivity, fueling your aspirations and nourishing your transformative mindset.

5.   Craft unyielding resilience amidst setbacks: Cultivate an indomitable spirit of resilience, poised to rise above setbacks and adversities. View setbacks as fleeting moments on your relentless pursuit of growth and adopt a mindset that transforms failures into potent steppingstones towards unparalleled success.

6.   Unleash the formidable might of gratitude: Embrace the potent practice of gratitude to redirect your focus towards the magnificent aspects of your existence. Express profound gratitude for the blessings, opportunities, and profound lessons that intertwine with your journey. Such a mindset shall amplify positive experiences and magnetize an abundance of positivity into your life.

7.   Immerse your subconscious in the vivid tapestry of visualization: Unleash the mesmerizing art of visualization to paint vivid scenes of the reality you yearn to manifest. Immerse yourself in the vibrant tapestry of your deepest desires, exuding the sensations and emotions of achieving your goals, surmounting obstacles, and reveling in a life of boundless fulfillment. Such a practice aligns the very fabric of your subconscious mind with your desired reality, rendering its manifestation all the more certain.

With these bold and audacious steps, you seize the reins of your destiny, unleashing the full potency of your mindset. Embrace the transformative power that rests within you, as you fearlessly script your journey towards resplendent triumph. The world shall tremble in awe as you dismantle limitations, manifest your infinite potential, and inscribe an extraordinary future that transcends all boundaries.

Chapter 14

The Ripple Effect: Making Waves in the World

Within the depths of our beings lies an untamed power to unleash a ripple effect that can shape the very fabric of our world. Brace yourself for an electrifying journey as we dive into the transformative force of our actions, choices, and contributions. Get ready to ignite a revolution of positive change and leave an indelible mark on the tapestry of humanity.

Each step, no matter how seemingly insignificant, possesses the potential to birth a resounding ripple that reverberates far and wide. By embracing the profound impact of our choices and aligning them with our deepest values, we become catalysts for transformative change in our communities, organizations, and the world at large.

As you journey through the chapters of this chapter, brace yourself for seismic moments of self-reflection and awakening. Prepare for the thunderous "ah-ha" moments that surge through your being as you unearth the depths of your unique gifts and strengths. Embrace these moments with resolute purpose and an unswerving commitment to unleashing a ripple effect that leaves an indomitable mark on the world.

Dear reader, you possess a symphony of potential to make a difference. By aligning your actions with your unwavering values and contributing to the greater good, you release a cataclysmic ripple effect that extends far beyond the confines of your immediate sphere of influence. Your contributions, no matter how seemingly small, possess the power to ignite a wildfire of positive change, reverberating through the annals of time.

The moment has arrived to unleash the tempest of your potential and surge forth with unwavering resolve to make a difference in the world. Embrace your distinct gifts, passions, and skills, wielding them as mighty weapons to uplift, inspire, and empower others. Your acts of kindness, your unwavering commitment to service, and your relentless pursuit of a positive legacy shall send forth ripples that transcend generations.

With every deliberate action, you conjure a tsunami of change that surges through the very fabric of our existence. Embrace the resplendent opportunity to forge a difference, both grand and minuscule, and let your actions serve as a testament to the resounding impact you wish to create. By leaving an indelible mark on the lives of others, you unfurl a tidal wave of transformation that transcends time itself.

Your Next 7 Steps

1. **Illuminate your values and ignite your purpose:** Delve deep within your soul to illuminate your unwavering values and ignite the blazing fire of your purpose. Clarify how you yearn to make an enduring impact on the world.

2. **Begin with bold acts of kindness:** Ignite the revolution of change by embarking on audacious acts of kindness in every facet of your life. Extend a helping hand to those in need, sow the seeds of compassion, and radiate positivity wherever you tread.

3. **Volunteer and be the ultimate benefactor:** Seek out opportunities to volunteer and magnanimously contribute your skills and resources to organizations and causes that resound with your values. By giving back, you not only make an extraordinary difference but also experience the euphoria of service and forge profound connections.

4. **Unleash the torrent of knowledge and expertise:** Channel the tempest of your knowledge, expertise, and experiences to inspire and empower others. Offer mentorship, pen thought-provoking articles or blog posts, or seize the stage to deliver captivating talks and workshops, thereby bestowing invaluable insights and lessons

5. **Be the harbinger of positive change:** Unleash your voice and become the harbinger of positive change. Speak up, take a bold stand for the issues that stir your soul. Wield your influence and galvanize

others to confront injustices, elevate awareness, and advocate for the transformative change our world so desperately needs.

6. **Foster collaboration and orchestrate unity:** Recognize the seismic power of collaboration and orchestrate the symphony of unity to amplify your impact. Seek out like-minded individuals and organizations, joining forces to magnify your efforts and achieve awe-inspiring results.

7. **Blaze the trail as an exemplar of change:** Embrace your role as an unwavering exemplar by embodying the values and actions you ardently wish to witness in the world. Lead with unyielding integrity, compassion, and empathy. Let your words, actions, and the resounding ripple effect you create in your own life inspire others to forge their own path of change.

With these explosive steps, you become the tempest that propels humanity towards an extraordinary future. Embrace the maelstrom of transformation that rests within you, as you fearlessly inscribe your legacy upon the world's tapestry. The world shall stand in awe as you dismantle limitations, manifest your boundless potential, and forever etch an indelible mark upon the annals of our existence.

Chapter 15

The Journey Unleashed: Igniting Limitless Growth

We've arrived at the epic finale of this life-altering expedition, where we boldly embrace the truth that the journey of growth and self-discovery knows no bounds. In this electrifying chapter, we unlock the secrets of embracing lifelong growth and unleash the explosive power it holds to propel us towards our boundless potential.

Throughout this extraordinary odyssey, we've dived deep into the realms of personal and professional growth, fearlessly exploring the landscapes of self-discovery, resilience, mindset, and making an indelible impact. These invaluable insights and lessons have been the launching pad for our ascent, but let us not forget—the journey continues, and the adventure never ends. The flame of growth shall forever burn bright within us.

Within the boundaries of this chapter, we shall embark on an audacious quest to unravel the essence of lifelong learning, unquenchable curiosity, and relentless improvement. We shall shatter the shackles of complacency, for it is through unyielding growth that we unlock the doors to our highest potential. By embracing the voyage of lifelong growth, we ensure that our path remains ablaze with passion, fulfillment, and alignment with our ever-evolving aspirations.

As you voyage through this climactic chapter, be prepared to embrace new horizons, to conquer uncharted territories, and to seize the untapped opportunities for growth that lie ahead. Explosive "ah-ha" moments shall illuminate your path as you bear witness to the transformative power of lifelong learning, as you revel in the pure joy that accompanies the acquisition of new knowledge and skills. Embrace these moments with an audacious spirit and an unwavering commitment to evolve and soar to new heights.

Dear reader, the journey of lifelong growth is an extraordinary gift—one that continues to bestow blessings upon us with each passing day. It serves as a testament to our unyielding dedication to personal and professional development, and as an unspoken vow to live a life teeming with purpose, impact, and fulfillment. By embracing lifelong growth, we unfurl our wings and take flight, ready to embrace new adventures, discoveries, and opportunities for self-expression.

The time has come to unleash the full force of our potential and boldly embrace the path that stretches before us. Let us pledge our unwavering allegiance to lifelong learning, curiosity that knows no bounds, and personal growth that transcends limitations. Let the journey of lifelong growth be an ode to our insatiable thirst for knowledge, an anthem of our commitment to continuous improvement, and a testament to the relentless belief in our unlimited potential.

As we conclude this book and march triumphantly into the unknown, let us acknowledge that growth is not a final destination but a perpetual voyage. Let us embrace the challenges that test our mettle, celebrate the victories that shape our character, and forever remain curious and open to the infinite possibilities that await. With every step, we shed our old skin and emerge as a reborn version of ourselves, and in turn, the world transforms around us.

The journey continues, dear reader, with unbridled vigor, with a spirit that defies gravity, and with an unwavering commitment to your personal and professional growth. The possibilities that lie ahead are infinite, and the potential within you is a tempest waiting to be unleashed. Embrace the journey, embrace the growth, and let your life be an awe-inspiring testament to the power of lifelong learning and the transformative impact it can have on your path to greatness

Your Next 7 Steps

1.   Blaze a trail of audacious learning goals: Set ablaze audacious learning goals that push the boundaries of your knowledge and skills. Whether it's acquiring new expertise or diving deeper into a subject that ignites your passion, embark on this lifelong learning journey with an unwavering commitment to growth.

2.   Conquer uncharted territories of wisdom: Seek out diverse perspectives and venture into uncharted territories of wisdom. Engage with individuals from various backgrounds, cultures, and fields, eager to absorb their experiences, ideas, and unconventional ways of thinking. Let curiosity guide you as you explore new frontiers of knowledge.

3.   Shatter the barriers of complacency with relentless curiosity: Unleash the force of relentless curiosity within you. Cultivate an insatiable thirst for knowledge that defies the status quo. Dare to ask questions, challenge assumptions, and venture into the realm of the unknown. Let curiosity be the fuel that propels you forward on your lifelong growth journey.

4.   Harness the power of failure as a catalyst for greatness: Embrace failure as an unwavering ally on your path to greatness. See each setback as an opportunity to gain invaluable insights, learn from your mistakes, and emerge stronger than before. Let failure be the catalyst that propels you towards your highest potential.

5.   Seek wisdom from sages and embrace mentorship: Seek the wisdom of sages who have tread the path of lifelong growth before you. Surround yourself with mentors who can provide guidance, support, and encouragement on your quest for self- improvement. Embrace their wisdom and let it fuel your journey towards greatness.

6.   Cultivate self-reflection and forge unbreakable self-awareness: Engage in the art of self-reflection to assess your progress, strengths, and areas for improvement. Cultivate a profound self-awareness that allows you to understand your motivations, values, and aspirations. Align your growth efforts with your authentic self, propelling you towards your true potential.

7.   Embrace the dynamic dance of change and adaptability: Embrace change as the heartbeat of growth and the catalyst for evolution. Remain adaptable in the face of new challenges and opportunities, eager to embrace innovation and seize the possibilities that lie before you. Let your ability to adapt become the cornerstone of your lifelong growth journey.

As you embark on this epic chapter, remember to infuse it with your distinctive boldness, your unstoppable spunk, and an unwavering belief in your ability to embrace lifelong growth and shape a destiny of extraordinary magnitude. The world awaits your unrivaled brilliance, your insatiable hunger for knowledge, and the seismic impact you are destined to make. Thank you for accompanying us on this extraordinary journey, dear reader. May your path be adorned with countless triumphant moments, unbounded growth, and an everlasting legacy that transcends the boundaries of time. The world has been forever transformed by your unwavering commitment to personal and professional growth.

With a resounding cheer and heartfelt gratitude,

Crystal Ellison

Author Bio

Crystal Ellison, a visionary entrepreneur. A fearless advocate for community equals connection, for personal empowerment, for breaking the chains in business. With a profound understanding of the transformative power of embracing one's gifts, Crystal Ellison has forged a path that others can follow to achieve remarkable success. From humble beginnings, Crystal has embarked on an incredible journey, determined to build a legacy that defied the odds. Faced with skeptics who believed her visions and steps were impossible, Crystal fearlessly pushed forward and proved that resilience, determination, and a strong belief in oneself can shatter any barriers.

The trademarked brand "PUSHMETAL" founded by Crystal, embodies the spirit of pushing beyond limits, challenging the status quo, and finding success in unconventional ways. This brand has become a beacon of inspiration for aspiring entrepreneurs, attracting a community of like-minded individuals eager to create their own path to success. However, Crystal's impact extends beyond the "PUSHMETAL" brand. Collaborating with her husband, Duane, they built the small niche business "CD Dents" from the ground up. In an industry where survival seemed improbable, their unwavering dedication, innovative thinking, and refusal to accept defeat allowed them to thrive.

In this e-book, Crystal delves deep into the core principles that have driven her remarkable journey. She passionately shares her insights on how community equals connection, helping readers discover the immense power of authentic relationships, collaboration, and support systems. Through the pages of this book, Crystal reveals the secrets to creating your "yes" moments, unlocking the potential within yourself, and harnessing your unique gifts to achieve unprecedented success. She offers invaluable guidance on breaking the chains in your business, encouraging readers to challenge conventional wisdom, take bold risks, and think outside the box. As a testament to her unwavering commitment to growth and personal development, Crystal emphasizes the importance of accountability. She reminds readers that the ultimate responsibility lies within themselves, and that by taking ownership of their actions and choices, they can manifest their dreams and transform their lives. Crystal empowers readers to recognize that the answers they seek are already within their grasp. She inspires individuals from all walks of life to embrace their unique talents, seize opportunities, and unleash their true potential. In this eye-opening e-book Crystal provides a roadmap for personal and professional growth, paving the way for readers to create a life that is rich with purpose, fulfillment, and limitless possibilities. Get ready to step into the spotlight and shine, because the answers you've been searching for are right in front of you.

Made in the USA
Middletown, DE
11 August 2023

36569122R00033